Pixabay image

A day at the
ZOO

MIKE ATNIP

ISBN: 978-1-943929-68-9

With the exception of the title page and pages 14–15, all photographs in this book are by Mike and Daniel Atnip.

Printed in China

Published by:
TGS International
P.O. Box 355, Berlin, Ohio 44610 USA
Phone: 330-893-4828 | Fax: 330-893-2305 | www.tgsinternational.com

TGS001448

Here we are at the zoo! We will get to see animals from all over the world. Look at this ostrich from Africa. It cannot fly, but it can outrun its enemies.

What do you want to see next?

Let's begin by watching the elephants. The zoo-keepers feed them hay. A large elephant will eat four or five bales of hay every day. Adults can weigh as much as two pickup trucks!

The zookeepers also feed the elephants fruits and vegetables. Watch how the elephant can pick up an apple with its trunk. The end of the trunk is so sensitive that it can pick up a single little peanut.

Look at the elephant's eye. What a little eye for such a large animal!

The giraffe is so tall that the zebra can walk right under its belly. It looks like this giraffe has worn the hair off its knee by kneeling down so often. Did you know that giraffes are the only animals born with horns, and that the horns are covered with hair?

The lion is known as the "king of the animals." If we watch him long enough, we may get to hear him roar! Lions, like most other cats, spend most of their day sleeping.

The Siberian tiger is the biggest wildcat in the world. Aren't you glad that a piece of glass is between him and us?

The snow leopard is a beautiful cat. Of the three cats we have looked at, I like it the best. Which cat do you like the best?

The red panda looks like it could be part raccoon, part bear, and part red fox. It sure looks cuddly! Red pandas eat a lot of bamboo just like panda bears do, but they are not actually pandas. They are more closely related to the skunk or raccoon.

Ring-tailed lemurs look like the red panda, but they are not pandas either. Which do you think is cuter, the red panda or the ring-tailed lemur?

Ring-tailed lemurs like to cuddle up into a ball. They look so fluffy, it makes you want to pet them. Lemurs are not monkeys, although they sometimes like to climb trees like monkeys.

Red ruffed lemurs
get their name from
the ruffs of bright red
hair around their
ears. They are very
clean and take lots
of time to pick dirt
and bugs out of their
fur and the fur of
other red ruffed
friends.

They love to climb trees,
like this one has done.
That's where they get their
favorite food—fruit!

15

This gorilla is resting. She is sitting like a human, and her hands look a lot like ours. But we are not related to gorillas. The Bible tells us in the book of Genesis that we came from Adam and Eve.

This gorilla has a comfy life. The animals at the zoo are well cared for and have plenty to eat. Some have been put in the zoo because they got hurt, and the zoo takes care of them.

American flamingos are often orange.
Do not try to bend your neck into a
figure eight like this one!

18

The greater flamingo is more pink. It is amazing how God can make birds and animals with so many colors.

Let's go look at the bears. Do you know which bear this is?

Yes, it's a polar bear! Polar bears have warm coats. They love to swim in ice-cold water.

This grizzly bear is taking a nap. While he is sleeping, let's look closely at the long claws on his front feet. Then we will examine his furry rear foot. The fur grows over his foot and toes to keep them warm.

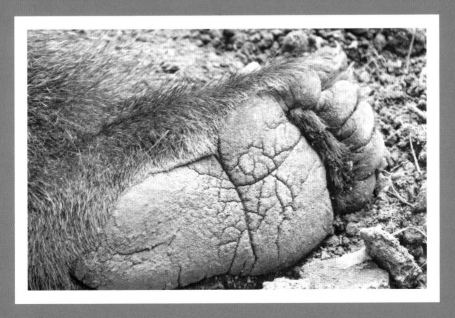

What do you think of the Galapagos tortoise? I don't think it would win any beauty contest! The zookeeper is not afraid to pet its head, but I would be scared to get my fingers close to its mouth.

Galapagos tortoises can live to be more than a hundred years old. This one is about thirty years old.

Like polar bears, penguins love to swim in icy waters. God designed them to survive in extremely harsh weather.

They are not very afraid of people, so it's easy to walk up to them, even in the wild. The colored bands on the wings are like name tags. They help the zookeepers know which penguin is which.

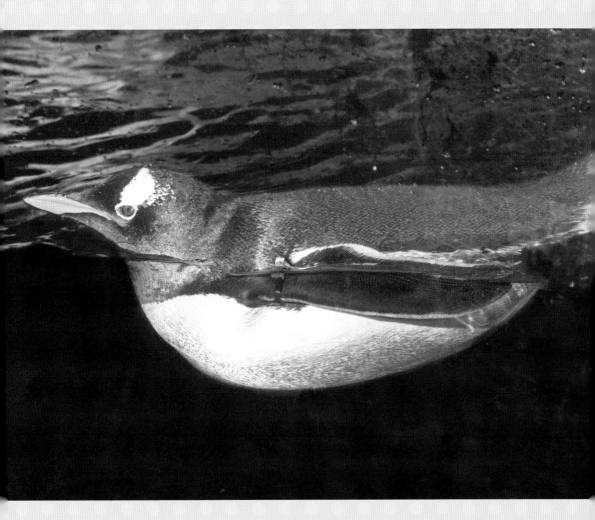

I wish this colobus monkey were active, but he does not want to play at the moment. His long white hairs look like a cape hanging over his shoulders.

Kangaroos have long tails too.
They use them like a third leg
to prop themselves up.

This rhinoceros looks tough. I wouldn't want to get into a fight with him! Rhinos have strong skin that can be up to two inches thick.

Like pigs, rhinos do not have sweat glands. They must roll in the mud to keep cool.

While the rhinoceros is big and strong, the dama gazelle is swift. What animal do you think would love to eat a dama gazelle for supper?

Turn the page to see!

Did you guess a leopard? Now you know why the dama gazelle needs to be so swift. I'm glad we do not need to worry about leopards trying to eat us. The top one is called a clouded leopard.

Let's go over to the snake building now.

The eyelash pit viper has "eyelashes" formed by scales sticking out above its eyes. Do you see the two black ones above this snake's eye? Eyelash pit vipers can be various colors. This yellow one is pretty even though it looks kind of mean.

This rattlesnake is from South America. I'm glad it's behind the glass because it looks ready to strike at us. If you ever see a rattlesnake outside, leave it alone. Rattlesnakes are venomous!

Have you ever seen the rattle of a rattlesnake? Many people say that the number of segments tells how many years old the snake is, but that is not true.

A rattlesnake gets another rattle segment
every time it sheds its skin, which can
happen several times in one year.

Komodo dragons have a name that sounds ferocious. However, they are just large lizards—the largest on earth. They can grow up to ten feet long. Their name comes from one of the islands where they are found: Komodo Island, Indonesia.

Let's look at one more reptile before we go to the birds. The day gecko can walk on walls. Since it has no eyelids, it cleans its eyes with its long tongue.

God gave the ibis a long, curved beak that it uses to dig into the mud for food. Did you notice that its head is bald like a turkey's?

The barn owl lives on every continent except Antarctica. It's heart-shaped face gives it a unique look. Some people call it the monkey-faced owl.

Let's make the river otters our last stop. I love to watch them swim and play. They seem to put on a show sometimes. I would like to be able to swim half as well as they can!

Well, that finishes our trip to the zoo. Which of God's marvelous creatures did you like the best?

About the Author

Mike Atnip, his wife Ellen, and their son Daniel live close to Clark, Ohio. Mike grew up among the cornfields of east-central Indiana, tromping through the fields and woods on a regular basis. Ellen grew up in southeast Pennsylvania, at the foot of Blue Mountain, but later lived in northern New York where the snow piles deep. Daniel was adopted from the tall Andes Mountains in Bolivia, South America, but has spent most of his life in the United States.

The desire of the Atnip family is that people young and old will see God's glory, power, and love in the creation of so many marvelous forms of life and submit their hearts to Him as to a loving Father and Friend.

Mike welcomes reader response and can be contacted at atnips@gmail.com. You may also write to him in care of Christian Aid Ministries, P.O. Box 360, Berlin, Ohio 44610.

Christian Aid Ministries

Christian Aid Ministries was founded in 1981 as a nonprofit, tax-exempt 501(c)(3) organization. Its primary purpose is to provide a trustworthy and efficient channel for Amish, Mennonite, and other conservative Anabaptist groups and individuals to minister to physical and spiritual needs around the world. This is in response to the command ". . . do good unto all men, especially unto them who are of the household of faith" (Galatians 6:10).

Each year, CAM supporters provide approximately 15 million pounds of food, clothing, medicines, seeds, Bibles, Bible story books, and other Christian literature for needy people. Most of the aid goes to orphans and Christian families. Supporters' funds also help to clean up and rebuild for natural disaster victims, put up Gospel billboards in the U.S., support several church-planting efforts, operate two medical clinics, and provide resources for needy families to make their own living. CAM's main purposes for providing aid are to help and encourage God's people and bring the Gospel to a lost and dying world.

CAM has staff, warehouses, and distribution networks in Romania, Moldova, Ukraine, Haiti, Nicaragua, Liberia, and Israel. Aside from management, supervisory personnel, and bookkeeping operations, volunteers do most of the work at CAM locations. Each year, volunteers at our warehouses, field bases, Disaster Response Services projects, and other locations donate over 200,000 hours of work.

CAM's ultimate purpose is to glorify God and help enlarge His kingdom. ". . . whatsoever ye do, do all to the glory of God" (1 Corinthians 10:31).

Creation to Redemption

God created plants, birds, and fish on the first five days. On the sixth day, He created land animals and man. At first man lived in harmony with God and the earth. But after Adam and Eve sinned, some people began to worship the creation rather than the Creator. Others began to selfishly destroy the creation in their pursuit of money, pleasure, or fame.

But God sent His Son Jesus into the world to rescue us from our sin. Jesus taught us to abandon the idolatry of nature worship and to be good stewards of God's creation. He died on the cross and rose again so we could be born again and enter the kingdom of God.

This kingdom of God is made up of those who have allowed Jesus to be King of their lives. Jesus leads these people into a harmonious relationship with God and teaches them to live holy, loving, and unselfish lives as they relate to people and things on this earth. They are in the world but not of the world and look forward to their final redemption in heaven.